CONTENTS

KU-520-212

NORTH AMERICA – A CONTINENT OF CONTRASTS

North America is a huge and spectacular continent, and one of the most varied. It is the third largest continent after Asia and Africa, covering about 24,200,000 sq km (9,341,000 sq miles) – roughly twice the size of Europe. North America includes Greenland (a self-governing territory of Denmark), and the countries of Canada, the

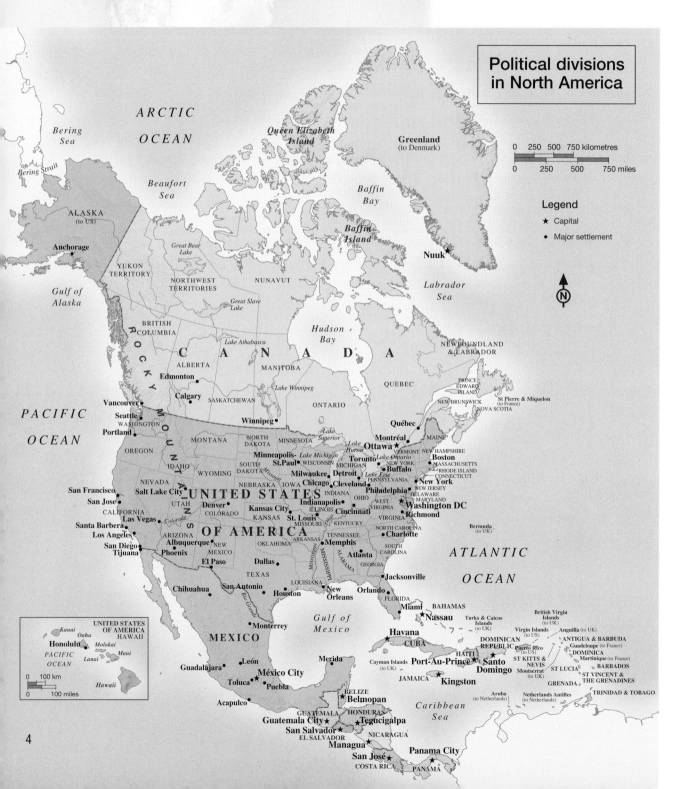

Political divisions in North America

ARCTIC OCEAN

Bering Sea

Bering Strait

Beaufort Sea

Queen Elizabeth Island

Greenland (to Denmark)

Baffin Bay

Baffin Island

Nuuk ★

Labrador Sea

0 250 500 750 kilometres
0 250 500 750 miles

Legend
★ Capital
● Major settlement

N

ALASKA (to US)

Anchorage

Gulf of Alaska

YUKON TERRITORY

Great Bear Lake

NORTHWEST TERRITORIES

NUNAVUT

Great Slave Lake

BRITISH COLUMBIA

Lake Athabasca

C A N A D A

Hudson Bay

NEWFOUNDLAND & LABRADOR

PACIFIC OCEAN

Edmonton

Calgary

ALBERTA

MANITOBA

SASKATCHEWAN

Lake Winnipeg

ONTARIO

QUEBEC

PRINCE EDWARD ISLAND

NEW BRUNSWICK

NOVA SCOTIA

St Pierre & Miquelon (to France)

Vancouver

Seattle

WASHINGTON

Portland

Winnipeg

OREGON

MONTANA

NORTH DAKOTA

MINNESOTA

Lake Superior

Québec

Montréal

MAINE

Ottawa ★

VERMONT

NEW HAMPSHIRE

Lake Huron

Minneapolis

St.Paul

WISCONSIN

IDAHO

WYOMING

SOUTH DAKOTA

Milwaukee

MICHIGAN

Lake Michigan

Toronto

Lake Ontario

Buffalo

Boston

MASSACHUSETTS

RHODE ISLAND

CONNECTICUT

NEW YORK

NEVADA

NEBRASKA

IOWA

Chicago

Detroit

Lake Erie

Cleveland

PENNSYLVANIA

New York

NEW JERSEY

San Francisco

Salt Lake City

UTAH

UNITED STATES

INDIANA

OHIO

Philadelphia

DELAWARE

MARYLAND

San Jose

Denver

COLORADO

Kansas City

KANSAS

St. Louis

Indianapolis

ILLINOIS

Cincinnati

WEST VIRGINIA

Washington DC

Richmond

CALIFORNIA

Las Vegas

Colorado

OF AMERICA

MISSOURI

KENTUCKY

VIRGINIA

Bermuda (to UK)

Santa Barbara

Los Angeles

ARIZONA

Albuquerque

NEW MEXICO

OKLAHOMA

ARKANSAS

TENNESSEE

Memphis

NORTH CAROLINA

Charlotte

San Diego

Tijuana

Phoenix

El Paso

Dallas

TEXAS

ALABAMA

GEORGIA

SOUTH CAROLINA

Atlanta

Mississippi

ATLANTIC OCEAN

Chihuahua

San Antonio

LOUISIANA

Houston

New Orleans

Jacksonville

Orlando

FLORIDA

Miami

Monterrey

Gulf of Mexico

BAHAMAS

Nassau ★

Turks & Caicos Islands (to UK)

British Virgin Islands (to UK)

Virgin Islands (to US)

Anguilla (to UK)

MEXICO

Havana ★

CUBA

DOMINICAN REPUBLIC

Puerto Rico (to US)

ANTIGUA & BARBUDA

Guadeloupe (to France)

DOMINICA

ST KITTS & NEVIS

Martinique (to France)

Guadalajara

León

Merida

Cayman Islands (to UK)

Port-Au-Prince ★

HAITI

Santo Domingo ★

Montserrat (to UK)

ST LUCIA

BARBADOS

México City ★

JAMAICA

Kingston ★

ST VINCENT & THE GRENADINES

GRENADA

Toluca

Puebla

BELIZE

Belmopan ★

Aruba (to Netherlands)

Netherlands Antilles (to Netherlands)

TRINIDAD & TOBAGO

Acapulco

GUATEMALA

HONDURAS

Caribbean Sea

Guatemala City ★

Tegucigalpa ★

San Salvador ★

EL SALVADOR

NICARAGUA

Managua ★

San José ★

Panama City ★

COSTA RICA

PANAMA

Hawaii inset

UNITED STATES OF AMERICA HAWAII

Kauai

Oahu

Honolulu

Molokai

Maui

PACIFIC OCEAN

Lanai

Hawaii

0 100 km
0 100 miles

United States and Mexico. For the purposes of this book, the islands of the Caribbean and countries of Central America as far south as Panama are also considered to be part of North America because of their close geographical, economic and political links with Mexico, the United States and Canada.

North America contains twenty-three independent countries. The United States and Mexico are both federal republics. Canada, Belize and eight Caribbean countries each have their own governments, but they recognize the British monarch, Queen Elizabeth II, as their head of state. The continent has ten democratic republics, including Costa Rica, Panama, and Trinidad and Tobago, and one Communist republic, Cuba. Fourteen territories connected to Britain, France, the United States and Denmark, such as Greenland and Martinique, are also included in the region.

PHYSICAL VARIETY

North America boasts the world's largest island, Greenland, which is 2,166,086 sq km (836,109 sq miles) in area, as well as Lake Superior – the biggest freshwater lake in the world. Lake Superior is one of the five Great Lakes (see page 18) which, along with their many connected rivers and waterways, account for one-fifth of the world's fresh water. In the United States, one of the world's most famous and spectacular natural features, the Grand Canyon, reaches a depth of 1.6 km (one mile). Running from north to south, the Western Cordillera is a vast mountain range that stretches from Alaska all the way to Panama in Central America. In Canada and the United States this range is known as the Rocky Mountains (the Rockies), in Mexico and Central America as the Sierra Madre.

A WEALTH OF WILDLIFE

North America's many differing landscapes offer habitats for a wide variety of wildlife. The continent is home to many well-known species including grizzly bears, coyotes, and birds such as the bald eagle and the rare Californian Condor. There are many exotic species, including jaguars in Central America, howler monkeys in Barbados and the Cuban pygmy frog. The coral reef of Belize is the world's fifth largest, and supports a great diversity of marine life. However, many of the species in Central America and the Caribbean are vulnerable to extinction or are critically endangered, largely due to population growth, urbanization and farming.

The jaguar is one of the most beautiful – and dangerous – mammals to live in the Belize rainforest.

1. THE HISTORY OF NORTH AMERICA

*T*HE EARLIEST PEOPLE TO SEE THE LAND THAT IS NOW **NORTH** America probably came from Asia about 15,000 years ago. At that time, the earth was experiencing an Ice Age, and so much water was locked into huge ice sheets that sea levels were about 175 m (575 feet) lower than today. It is generally believed that the Bering Strait – a narrow passage in the far north that separates North America and Asia – was not covered by sea during that time, creating a land bridge between the two continents.

This pyramid at Kukulcan is just one of the many Mayan sites found across much of Central America.

EARLY SETTLERS

These early peoples were hunters and gatherers, and they gradually moved south to warmer climates. In some places they began to grow food and to settle. They are believed to be the ancestors of most Native Americans. One exception is the Inuit of the far north. The Inuit are believed to have descended from Asian ancestors who had adapted to living in very cold climates, hunting caribou (reindeer), seals and even whales. They probably travelled by boats along the coastlines of the Arctic Ocean about 5,000 years ago. Instead of going south, they travelled east, and eventually settled in Greenland. The Inuit still live in parts of Alaska, Canada and Greenland.

FACT FILE

The term 'Inuit' refers to the people inhabiting the Arctic coast of North America. The term 'eskimo,' which means 'eater of raw meat', is now considered offensive.

CENTRAL AMERICA AND THE CARIBBEAN

Some groups of people settled in the Caribbean and Central America. For example, the Arawaks were found on most of the Caribbean islands. They practised shifting cultivation, a type of farming in which farmers grow crops on a piece of land until it is no longer productive, then abandon the land and move on to a new area. In about 1300, the Arawaks were driven out of many Caribbean islands by the Caribs who came from the northern coast of South America.

On mainland Central America, the Maya Indians lived in the Yucatán Peninsula of Mexico from about 2600BC. They spread into Guatemala, Belize and western Honduras. Another important people, the Aztecs, migrated from northern Mexico into the Valley of Mexico in the 1100s. In 1325 the Aztecs began to reclaim lake marshland to build their capital on the site occupied today by Mexico City.

FACT FILE

Excavations of the Viking settlement at L'Anse aux Meadows National Historic Site in Newfoundland began in 1961. The archaeological remains of the earliest known European settlement in North America were declared a United Nations World Heritage Site in 1978.

VIKINGS

Even during this early period of settlement there was a European presence in North America. Around the middle of the 10th century, Vikings from Denmark, Sweden and Norway built settlements and traded along Canada's coastline between Newfoundland and Baffin Island. They used wood from Newfoundland to build boats and houses in Greenland.

The remains of the first Viking settlement in Newfoundland are found at L'Anse aux Meadows National Historic Site.

THE COLONIAL PERIOD

Europeans began settling in North America in the late 1400s and early 1500s. Britain, France, Spain and Portugal were all eager to exploit North America's reputed resources and to control territories in the 'New World', as it became known.

veyotlipan. çonca qnamicoqz mtlatoque qmaca ǵyxǵchqualom.

Aztecs present gifts to the Spanish *conquistador*, Hernan Cortes, who went on to conquer the Aztec Empire.

Explorers from Spain reached the Caribbean in 1492 and Central America in 1501. Spanish *conquistadors*, or conquerors, invaded Central America and fought the native peoples. By 1525, the Spanish controlled much of the region. The *conquistadors* also brought with them diseases such as smallpox and measles which were previously unknown in North America. The native peoples had no immunity to these diseases, and within 100 years nearly 90 per cent of the indigenous (native) population in the Caribbean and Central America had been wiped out by disease.

French and British settlers began to arrive off the coasts of present-day Canada and the United States from around 1600. A permanent settlement was established in Virginia in 1607 and came to be known as Jamestown. The settlement at Jamestown became profitable for a reason that nobody had foreseen – tobacco. Tobacco was grown widely by Native Americans, and they introduced it to the Europeans. At first used as an important medicine, tobacco quickly became a valuable cash crop in Virginia, with most of the crop being exported to Britain.

INDEPENDENCE AND MANIFEST DESTINY

In 1775, thirteen American colonies went to war against Britain. Many American colonists resented the high taxes that Britain imposed on them, particularly as they had no representation in the British parliament. In 1776, the colonists

FACT FILE

An Italian sailor named Christopher Columbus was the first European to set eyes on what is now Cuba, Haiti and the Dominican Republic, in 1492. Columbus claimed these lands for Spain, the country sponsoring his voyage. He was actually trying to find a westward sea passage to India and the Far East!

FACT FILE

France and Britain wrestled for control over St Lucia between 1605 and 1814. Power changed hands fourteen times before the British finally gained control of the island.

issued a Declaration of Independence, marking the birth of the United States of America. The war, known as the American Revolution, continued until 1783, when Britain finally recognized the new country.

Ever since the arrival of the first Europeans, relations between settlers and Native Americans had been uneasy and sometimes hostile. As the United States expanded during the 1800s, a philosophy known as Manifest Destiny was often used to justify

●●●●●●● ➤ IN FOCUS: Slavery and the Civil War

Black people from Africa were originally brought to North America to work as slaves on plantations. The slave trade from Africa to the Caribbean and the United States brought some 13-14 million Africans to the region in the 1700s. Slavery became a vital part of the economies of the Caribbean and the southern states of the United States. In these regions, slaves provided the labour force for plantations growing cotton, sugar, and tobacco.

During the 1800s, the issue of slavery caused the United States to split in two. Many people in the richer, industrial north became opposed to slavery and called for its abolition. However, people in the southern states

wanted to defend their prosperous agricultural way of life – which was based on slavery. Starting in 1860, the southern states formally withdrew from the Union to form the Confederate States of America. Fighting between Union and Confederate forces began in 1861. The bitter and bloody American Civil war lasted for four years. It ended with victory for the Union forces and the abolition of slavery throughout the country.

A slave family at work on a cotton plantation near Savannah, Georgia, in the southern United States.

the treatment of Native Americans. The idea of Manifest Destiny was that white Americans had the right to spread across and possess the continent of North America – even if this meant killing Native Americans or forcing them off their lands.

CHANGE AND REVOLUTION IN CENTRAL AMERICA

Spanish rule in Central America came to an end in the 1820s. The United Provinces of Central America was formed in 1823, but by 1839 this union had split into the independent states of Guatemala, Honduras, El Salvador, Nicaragua and Costa Rica. Throughout much of the 20th century these states had numerous internal disputes, experiencing military takeovers as well as civil wars. Since the 1980s, however, there has been a general trend towards democratically elected governments.

Nicaragua, for example, experienced more than four decades of dictatorship under the Somoza family. This rule came to an end in 1978 with the Sandinista Revolution. Eleven years of civil war followed between the Sandinistas and their opponents, the Contras – former members of the National Guard who had supported the Somoza regime. The Contras were backed by the United States which was suspicious about the close links between the Sandinistas and the Communist regime in Cuba, and which wanted to destabilize the Sandinista government.

The Contras finally disbanded in 1990. Although the Sandinistas won democratic elections in 1985, they were defeated in 1990, 1996 and 2001. Since 1990, Nicaragua has been politically stable. However, its fragile economy, shattered by years of civil war, received a further setback when the country was badly hit by Hurricane Mitch in 1998.

FACT FILE

Between 1979 and 1991, civil war in El Salvador claimed the lives of over 75,000 people.

Sandinista rebels arrive in the capital of Nicaragua, Managua, to take control of the government on 20 June 1979.

INDEPENDENCE IN THE CARIBBEAN

During the world economic depression of the 1930s, the Caribbean islands experienced high levels of unemployment. Demands for independence were urged by labour movements on many of the islands. The British responded by allowing self-government, the French incorporated the islands more closely into the French economy, and the Dutch permitted more self-rule.

After World War II, Britain tried to be free of its responsibilities to its Caribbean colonies by creating a single federal state – the West Indies Federation – which represented dozens of islands scattered over 3,200 km (1,990 miles) of ocean. Jamaica was the first island to leave the Federation in 1961, followed closely by Trinidad. Both became independent states in 1962. Barbados gained independence in 1966 and the other smaller islands, such as Dominica, Grenada and St Kitts, gradually followed suit.

Jamaica was the first British colony to become independent in 1962, an event commemorated in the annual Independence Day Parade in Charlestown.

CANADA

Canada remains part of the British Commonwealth, but there are separatist movements within Canada. For example, in 1976 French Canadians gained control of the province of Québec. In the following year, a law was passed to make French the official language of the province. In 1992, a self-governing homeland for the Inuit population was approved, and in 1999 that territory, Nunavut, was established out of the Northwest Territories.

FACT FILE

Nunavut, the Inuit homeland established in 1999, covers nearly one-quarter of Canada's land area.

THE UNITED STATES IN THE 20TH CENTURY

During the 20th century, the United States, Europe, large parts of Asia and other Pacific Rim countries were involved in two devastating world wars. The United States entered World War I (1914-18) in 1917, following the sinking of US ships by German submarines. The United States became involved in World War II in 1941, after Japan bombed Pearl Harbor in Hawaii, the home of the US Pacific naval fleet. The United States and its allies were victorious in the European fighting in May 1945. The end of the war in the Pacific came about four months later, with the surrender of Japan several days after the United States dropped atomic bombs on the Japanese cities of Hiroshima and Nagasaki.

The explosion of the atomic bomb at Hiroshima, Japan, on 6 August 1945. Three days later the United States dropped another atomic bomb on the Japanese city of Nagasaki.

FACT FILE

Hawaii was annexed by the United States in 1898 and became a US territory in 1900, making all its residents US citizens. It became the 50th state in 1959.

For the next forty-five years, the United States and the Union of Soviet Socialist Republics (USSR), the world's two 'superpowers', were engaged in an intense hostility and rivalry known as the Cold War. This power struggle was a response by the United States and its Western allies to the spread and influence of Communism. Although the Cold War was not a 'war' in the usual sense, the United States did become involved in conflicts such as the Korean War (1950-3) and the Vietnam War (1964-75). The end of the Cold War came after the reunification of Germany following the tearing down of the Berlin Wall in 1989, and the collapse of the political systems in many Communist countries, including the Soviet Union (1991).

Opinions about the involvement of the United States in world affairs are divided. Critics debate whether it has provided strong leadership or whether it has interfered in the internal affairs of other countries, such as in conflicts in the Middle

East, Bosnia, the Gulf states, and in Iraq. During the late 20th and early 21st centuries, the United States has also been the target of terrorist attacks, both at home and abroad. People responsible for the attacks often believe that the United States does not have the right to be involved in making decisions that affect other countries, and should not have a physical presence in these countries.

US soldiers stand guard in Baghdad, the capital of Iraq, in 2003. Since 1945, the United States has played a major role in world affairs.

CUBA

In 1959, Cuban dictator Fulgencio Batista was overthrown in a revolution led by a young lawyer, Fidel Castro. Castro established a Communist government and seized US businesses in Cuba, putting them under Cuban government control. In response, the United States banned trade with Cuba and cut off diplomatic relations. In 1962, there were reports that the Soviet Union was constructing nuclear missile launch-sites in Cuba, capable of launching attacks on US cities. The United States responded with a naval blockade of Cuba, demands that the launch-sites be removed and a threat of nuclear retaliation against the Soviet Union. During the crisis that followed the world stood on the edge of nuclear war, until the Soviet Union agreed to turn back ships carrying nuclear missiles to Cuba, and to take down the launch-sites.

Cuba continued to receive aid from the Soviet Union until the collapse of Communism in the late 1980s and early 1990s, when the aid dried up. As trade with the former Soviet Union also slumped, Cuba's economy suffered greatly. In addition, Cuba is still subject to US sanctions. Economic growth is slow (just over 1 per cent in 2003) and is fuelled mainly by tourism and from money sent back to Cuba from Cubans living abroad.

FACT FILE

In 2003, a total of about 2,500 Cubans attempted to leave Cuba for the United States by crossing the Straits of Florida in boats. The US Coast Guard turned back about 60 per cent of these people.

2. NORTH AMERICAN ENVIRONMENTS

NORTH AMERICA HAS A HUGE RANGE OF ENVIRONMENTS FROM POLAR deserts to sub-tropical forests, from coastal coral to mangroves, from lofty mountain peaks to rolling grasslands. There are many islands that have unique flora and fauna, as well as vast river networks and wetlands.

The Sierra Madre mountains were formed by tectonic forces that pushed up the limestone strata into near vertical layers.

FACT FILE

In Hawaii, the submarine volcano Loihi, which lies 1,000 m (3,280 feet) beneath the sea, is adding lava and building upwards to become the next Hawaiian island – in about 10,000 years.

TECTONICS AND THE ENVIRONMENT

The movement of the plates that make up the earth's crust is known as plate tectonics. Tectonic movements have played a major role in the formation of some of the mountainous environments in North America. Where two plates meet, the denser plate plunges beneath (subducts) the less dense plate and pushes the ground upwards. This force has helped to create mountain ranges such as the Rocky Mountains and the Sierra Madre, as well as the rugged Cordillera de Talamanca of Central America. Tectonic activity also explains the existence of volcanoes such as Mount St Helens in the United States, Volcán Pacaya in Guatemala and the Hawaiian Islands in the Pacific. Mount St Helens and Volcán Pacaya are situated on plate boundaries, where magma – molten rock from the interior of the earth – breaks through to the surface. Magma can also rise to the surface underneath a plate, to form a hot spot. The Hawaiian Islands have been formed as the Pacific plate has moved slowly over a hot spot, creating a series of volcanoes.

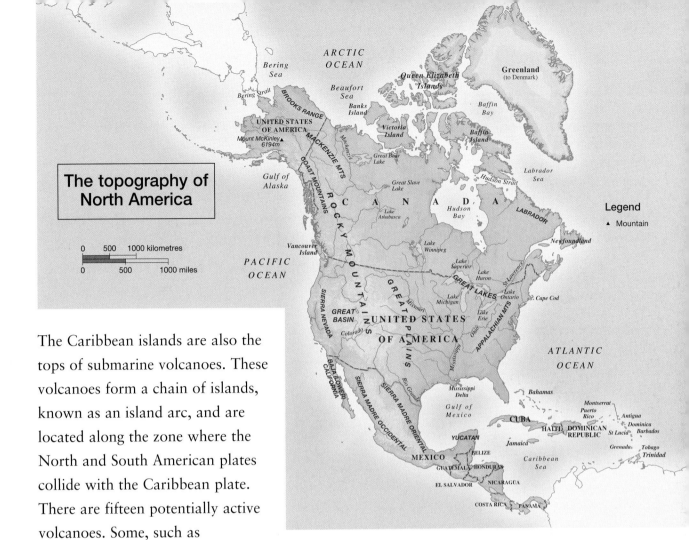

The topography of North America

Legend
▲ Mountain

The Caribbean islands are also the tops of submarine volcanoes. These volcanoes form a chain of islands, known as an island arc, and are located along the zone where the North and South American plates collide with the Caribbean plate. There are fifteen potentially active volcanoes. Some, such as Montserrat, are above ground while others, such as Kick 'em Jenny north of Grenada, are submerged beneath the sea. The volcanoes that form the oldest islands of the Caribbean – Jamaica, Hispaniola and Cuba – are no longer active.

●●●●●●● ▶ IN FOCUS: Living with the Volcano

The eruption of the Soufriére Hills volcano on the island of Montserrat began in 1995. In 1997 clouds of superheated ash and gas, called pyroclastic flows, killed nineteen people and covered Plymouth (the capital city) in ash and mudflows. Montserrat's only airport was destroyed, and the southern half of the island was declared unsafe. Since 2000, many people have returned to Montserrat, and there has been much rebuilding in the northern part of the island. But volcanologists (people who study volcanoes) do not know whether the Soufriére Hills volcano will continue to erupt for another six – or six hundred – years!

FACT FILE

The largest earthquakes ever to affect North America were the three New Madrid earthquakes of 1811-12, so-called because they were on a fault line near the town of New Madrid, Missouri. They measured at least 8.0 on the Richter Scale and caused large areas of the earth to sink, new lakes to form, and the Mississippi River to change its course.

FACT FILE

North America's highest point is Mt McKinley (Denali) in Alaska, at 6,194 m (20,320 feet).

The flat wheat fields of North Dakota are part of the Great Plains – the 'bread-basket' of the world.

EARTHQUAKES

In some places, two plates slide horizontally against each other. This is called a fault line, and the movement of the earth's crust along a fault can cause both small and large earthquakes. The world's most famous fault line is the San Andreas Fault that runs through California for 1,125 km (700 miles). Notable earthquakes along this fault include the 1906 earthquake in San Francisco and the 1994 Northridge earthquake in Los Angeles, both of which brought great destruction to the region. The 1906 earthquake registered over 8.0 on the Richter Scale, seven hundred people were killed and much of the city was destroyed by fire. In 1994, the earthquake measured 6.6 on the Richter Scale, sixty people were killed and the damage was estimated at over US$15 billion.

HIGH AND LOW LAND

North America has many dramatic mountains and areas of high elevation. More than half of Mexico is located 1,000 m (3,200 feet) above sea level. The Mexican plateau runs from north to south through the country. In the north it forms a dry desert, while further south the land rises and becomes more mountainous. The increase in altitude leads to a decrease in temperature and the Central Highlands are about 10°C (18°F) cooler than the northern desert. One-third of Central America is over 1,000 m (3,200 feet) in height. There are relatively few low-lying areas, but some of these are found along the Pacific and Caribbean coastlines, around lakes Nicaragua and Managua, and in the northern part of Guatemala. In the centre of the United States and Canada are the central lowlands, which include the Great Plains. The central lowlands are bounded by higher ground.

Towards the east coast are the Appalachian Mountains, characterized by low, rounded ridges and gentle valleys, while towards the west are the Rockies.

RIVERS AND LAKES

North America contains one of the world's largest and most important river basins. The Mississippi (3,765 km; 2,339 miles) and Missouri (4,023 km; 2,500 miles) rivers drain the area between the Appalachians and the Rockies – over half of North America. The Mississippi and its valley are important for transport, agriculture and industry. The rivers on the western side of North America, such as the Columbia and Fraser rivers which flow between the Western Cordillera range of mountains and the Pacific Ocean, are shorter in length but impressive in stature. Many of these rivers have eroded deep canyons, such as Fraser Canyon in British Columbia. The Colorado River cuts through the Rockies and continues into northern Arizona, where it has carved through rock over 2,000 million years old to form the Grand Canyon. With a depth of 1.6 km (one mile) from its rim, the Grand Canyon is 350 km (217 miles) long and 6-29 km (4-18 miles) wide. Canyons have become important locations for the building of large dams, a source of hydroelectric power (see page 38). The lakes behind these dams are used as reservoirs and for recreation.

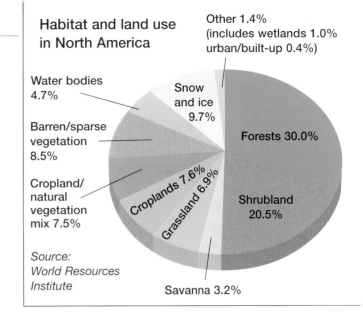

Habitat and land use in North America

Other 1.4% (includes wetlands 1.0% urban/built-up 0.4%)
Water bodies 4.7%
Snow and ice 9.7%
Barren/sparse vegetation 8.5%
Forests 30.0%
Cropland/natural vegetation mix 7.5%
Croplands 7.6%
Grassland 6.9%
Shrubland 20.5%
Savanna 3.2%

Source: World Resources Institute

The Colorado River has carved its way through rock to reveal 2,000 million years of geological history in the Grand Canyon.

Water rights have always been an important factor in the development of North America. There is an ongoing debate about whether fresh water from the Great Lakes should be made available to other states outside the Great Lakes basin. An agreement known as Annex 2001 attempts to limit water usage from the lakes to local communities. Water rights are especially controversial in this part of North America because the Great Lakes are used for more than drinking water or irrigation. They are vital to the region's manufacturing, as well as its tourism and recreation.

Pressure to divert water outside the region is likely to come from the United States rather than Canada, as Canada has vast water resources on which to draw and a much smaller population than the United States.

Metropolitan Chicago overlooks Lake Michigan.

FACT FILE

The St Lawrence River and the Great Lakes cover 245,000 sq km (94,600 sq miles) and form a vast store of water which is a vital resource for drinking water, recreation, industry, transport and trade for large areas of the United States and Canada.

The five Great Lakes are another major natural feature which have an important economic function. Four of the Great Lakes – Superior, Huron, Erie and Ontario – lie on the boundary between the United States and Canada, while one – Lake Michigan – lies completely within the United States. The Great Lakes drain out to the Gulf of St Lawrence and the Atlantic Ocean through the St Lawrence River.

WATER BOUNDARIES
Rivers and waterways help to mark the boundaries between the different countries of North America. The Niagara Falls forms part of the boundary between the United States and Canada.

The American Falls are 51 m (167 feet) high and 330 m (1,083 feet) wide, while the Horseshoe Falls in Canada are 49 m (161 feet) high and 790 m (2,592 feet) wide. In Central America, the Rio Grande River (3,034 km; 1885 miles) forms part of the boundary between the United States and Mexico, and the Usumacinta River (965 km; 600 miles) is part of the border between Mexico and Guatemala.

The islands of the Caribbean have relatively short rivers. Some islands have very few rivers, notably Barbados which is formed of permeable limestone but which has a substantial reservoir of groundwater beneath the surface providing an important source of fresh water.

HUMAN IMPACT ON RIVERS AND LAKES

Humans have long manipulated rivers and lakes for their own gain. Rivers have been widened, straightened, deepened, dammed, and channelized. For example, engineering works on the Mississippi have shortened the river by 270 km (168 miles) by removing some of its meanders (bends). But in recent years there has been a movement to restore some rivers to their natural state. The aim is to improve water quality by using vegetation and soil to filter pollutants from the water, as well as allowing floodplains to soak up flood waters. One example is the Kissimmee River in Florida, where over 100 sq km (39 sq miles) of river and floodplain are being restored at a cost of over US$400 million. The first phase was completed in 2001, but the future of the project is uncertain due to a shortage of funding.

FACT FILE

As the Rio Grande River flows from the Rockies to the Gulf of Mexico it is reduced to a trickle by irrigation demands.

River engineers have reintroduced the meanders to the Kissimmee River in Florida.

CLIMATE AND WEATHER

The continent of North America stretches from the Arctic Circle almost to the Equator. Combined with the influence of the continent's many different landscapes and the effects of the Pacific and Atlantic oceans, North America has an incredibly varied range of climates and temperatures.

Deep within the Arctic Circle, temperatures rise above freezing point for only a few months of the year. In the Arctic, winter temperatures may be as low as -25°C (-13°F) and summer temperatures reach only 8°C (46°F). By contrast, in Cuba the average temperature in January is as high as 21°C (70°F), and the average temperature in July is 30°C (86°F).

Rainfall across the continent is particularly varied. Areas that receive less than 250 mm (10 inches) of rain each year are termed deserts. In North America there are many desert areas such as the Sonoran Desert (Mexico and Arizona) and Death Valley (California). There are also cold deserts such as Greenland. Rainfall is high along the Pacific coast of North America, and in Central America and the Caribbean. Much of the Caribbean, the countries of Central America, and the south and southeast coasts of the United States experience hurricanes and tropical storms between June and November. The driest parts of North America are in the interior.

There is a clear link between climate and ecosystems. In the far north, where conditions are coldest, tundra grasslands occur. Moving south, across much of southern Alaska and Canada coniferous forests are found in areas that have significant snowfalls in winter but warm summers.

FACT FILE

In 2004, three hurricanes, Charley, Frances and Ivan, battered the Caribbean and the United States causing over forty deaths and extensive damage to Grenada, the Cayman Islands, Jamaica, Cuba and Florida.

A flooded house on the coast of western Cuba takes a battering from Hurricane Ivan in 2004. Much of the Caribbean and the southeast coast of the United States is vulnerable to hurricane damage.

Broadleaved, deciduous forests (which lose their leaves in winter) are found in warmer areas such as the northeastern United States, while grasslands flourish in the drier lands of the interior, such as the Great Plains. In southern California, Mediterranean conditions (warm, wet winters and hot, dry summers) produce Mediterranean woodland and chapparal (a type of Mediterranean shrub vegetation). In Central America and the Caribbean, the tropical climate is ideal for the rainforests that cover the region. The effect of the mountains in Costa Rica is to change the rainforest into cloud forest, as near-permanent clouds shroud the forest in mist.

Mount McKinley provides a stunning backdrop to this tundra landscape in Denali National Park, Alaska.

The pattern of weather in North America appears to be changing. It is possible that increases in hurricane activity and strength, and changes in the El Niño circulation of ocean currents, may be linked to global warming – the increase in temperatures throughout the world that is caused largely by the burning of fossil fuels. Any reduction in the burning of fossil fuels, however, may come at the expense of economic growth in North America.

FACT FILE

In the tornadoes that affect the central part of North America, winds can reach up to 480 km/h (300 mph).

3. THE PEOPLE OF NORTH AMERICA

NORTH AMERICA HAS A POPULATION OF AROUND 500 MILLION. ON THE whole, North America is one of the most sparsely populated regions in the world, with an average of only 22.5 people per sq km (58.4/sq mile).

DISTRIBUTION AND DENSITY

The distribution of population in North America is very uneven. Densities range from 1,185 people per sq km (3,048/sq mile) in Bermuda to three people per sq km (8/sq mile) in Canada. Over half of the population of North America lives in the United States. In the US states of Massachusetts and Connecticut, densities are over 100 people per sq km (256/sq mile), whereas in Colorado and New Mexico there are generally fewer than ten people per sq km (26/sq mile). There are some areas of very high population density, for example the urban sprawls of Los Angeles in California and Mexico City in Mexico. Moreover, some cities in the southern and western United States are among the fastest growing in North America, thanks to a trend for people to move to warmer areas. There are rapidly expanding cities in Nevada, Arizona and California, particularly in places where there is a concentration of high-tech industry, such as in San Jose in California and Phoenix in Arizona (see page 29).

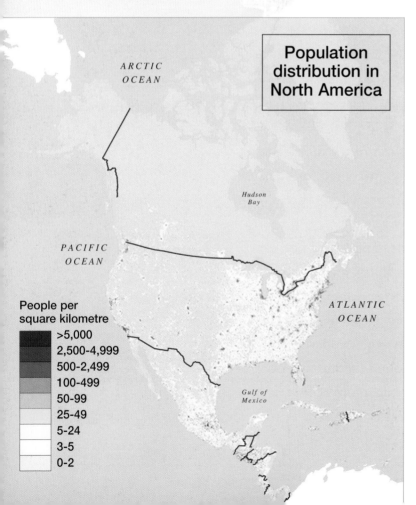

Population distribution in North America

ARCTIC OCEAN

PACIFIC OCEAN

ATLANTIC OCEAN

Hudson Bay

Gulf of Mexico

People per square kilometre
- >5,000
- 2,500-4,999
- 500-2,499
- 100-499
- 50-99
- 25-49
- 5-24
- 3-5
- 0-2

NATIVE AMERICANS

Indigenous population groups in North America include the Inuit, Aleut, Cherokee, Navajo, Chippewa, Sioux and Pueblo. Their distribution is very uneven, and they are often less well-off economically than their white counterparts.

Native American students improve their IT skills at Spokane Indian Reservation, United States.

Originally there were hundreds of Native American tribes. There are disputes regarding the size of the Native American population in 1500 – estimates range between 1.1 million and 12 million people. By 1900, however, the Native American population was only 237,000. The main cause of this genocide was disease, which accounted for up to 90 per cent of the deaths. Native Americans had their own rich and varied cultures and traditions. They also made valuable contributions to white American society, for example by introducing early settlers to crops such as maize, beans and squash, and sharing knowledge of traditional medicines. Today there are over 2 million Native Americans in the United States, with about 800,000 living on reservations and 1.2 million residing in urban areas. There are also approximately 300 Federal Indian reservations and 500 federally recognized tribes in the United States.

FACT FILE

One-third of foreign-born people in the United States live in the cities of Los Angeles and New York.

MIGRATION AND IMMIGRATION

One of the key characteristics of North America's population is migration. Immigration into North America from countries outside the region is also important. The 'brain drain' from Europe and Asia illustrates this trend. In 1961, 75 per cent of Canada's immigrants came from Europe, and 12 per cent from the United States. By 2000, over 50 per cent of Canada's immigrants came from Asia. Highly qualified workers, such as doctors, are drawn to North America by the lure of well-paid jobs.

FACT FILE

Most of the people on fixed-term visas, which allow foreigners with technical qualifications to work in the United States, come from India.

Compared with its rich northern neighbour, Mexico has a relatively low standard of living, insufficient jobs, and poorer education and health systems. Estimates suggest that each year between one and two million Mexicans try to cross into the United States. Although Mexican workers are a drain on America's social programs and benefits, they are essential to the nation's economy. The immigrants take the harder, dirtier, seasonal, more monotonous, more dangerous, less-skilled and lower-paid jobs. Despite the low pay by American standards, some immigrants can earn more during three or four months in the United States than in a full year in Mexico. Within Mexico, most immigrants have left the countryside to seek work in the cities. In turn, Mexico receives immigrants from its poorer neighbours to the south, such as El Salvador and Guatemala.

French is the official language in Québec province, Canada.

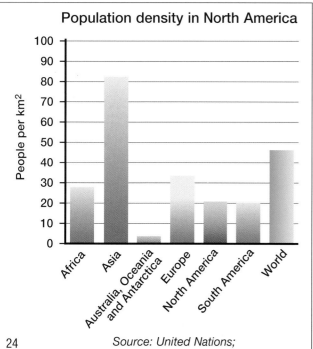

Population density in North America

Source: United Nations;
Britannica Book of the Year 2004

RACE AND ETHNICITY

More than 70 per cent of North Americans are descendants of Europeans. More than one-third of the population of the United States, and nearly half the population of Canada, have ancestors from Great Britain. More than one-quarter of Canadians have French ancestors. In the United States, there is also a significant number of people from Germany, Italy, Poland, and eastern European and Scandinavian countries. The European ancestors of Central Americans mostly came from Spain.

African Americans make up 12 per cent of the population of the United States. They are largely descended from slaves who were brought over from Africa to work in plantations in the south (see page 9). After the abolition of slavery in 1865, and throughout the 20th century, many African Americans moved north in search of new opportunities and higher-paying jobs in cities such as New York, Chicago and Detroit.

Most of the people of the Caribbean islands are also descended from black Africans. However, this varies between the islands. Although the native Caribs were almost completely wiped out by the early colonists, about 3,000 Caribs still live on the east side of Dominica, and there are smaller Carib populations on St Vincent and Trinidad. Other people in the Caribbean are of mixed black and white descent. In Barbados and Montserrat, for example, there are descendants of Irish slaves or convicts who mixed with indigenous peoples.

Many of the people of Mexico and Central America are *mestizos*, people of mixed white and Native American ancestry. *Mestizos* account for about 50 per cent of Central America's population, and up to 90 per cent of the population of El Salvador. The exception is Costa Rica, which has a predominantly white population. By contrast, Native Americans account for only 20 per cent of the population of Central America, although 60 to 70 per cent of the population in Guatemala is Native American.

Asians make up a small but growing percentage of North America's population. In 2000, 4.3 per cent of US residents were Asian, an increase of 65 per cent since 1990. Asians began emigrating to the continent in the 1800s and have come mainly from China, Japan, Korea and the Philippines. There is a large concentration of Asians in California and in Hawaii. More than two-thirds of Hawaii's population consists of 'Pacific Island population' – non-white people including Pacific islanders and those of Asian descent.

People from many different ethnic backgrounds have made their homes in the United States.

FACT FILE

In Belize, Honduras and Guatemala, a distinct ethnic group – the Garifuna – is descended from Caribs and black slaves from Africa.

FACT FILE

There are only about 136,000 Inuits and Aleuts (people related to the Inuits) in North America. They live in Alaska, northern Canada and Greenland.

The civil rights movement was a campaign for equal rights for black citizens of the United States which started in the mid 1950s. The most famous civil rights leader was Dr Martin Luther King Jr. When the movement began, segregation laws in the southern states of the United States separated black and white people in all areas of life – in schools, in theatres, on public transport. Black people were treated like second-class citizens. After a long and bitter struggle, the Civil Rights Act was passed in 1964 forbidding segregation in public places. Black people gained equal voting rights the following year. Dr King was assassinated in 1968. Despite legislation, racial discrimination and prejudice still exists among people in many parts of the United States, as well as in other parts of North America.

Black Americans have fought long and hard for racial equality.

FACT FILE

The proportion of people living on less than US$2 per day in North America varies from 45 per cent in El Salvador and 44.4 per cent in Honduras, to 24.3 per cent in Mexico, 14.3 per cent in Costa Rica and less than 2 per cent in Cuba. (Figures for Canada and the United States are not recorded.)

QUALITY OF LIFE

The quality of life varies enormously across North America. Residents of Canada have the highest life expectancy in North America at 79 years. Average life expectancy is also high in the United States (76 years), Barbados (77 years) and Bermuda (77 years). In contrast, life expectancy in Haiti is only 53 years. High life expectancies are partly the result of good living conditions, such as clean water, proper sanitation and sufficient food, and partly a result of government investment in health care. The United States spends 12.9 per cent of its Gross Domestic Product (GDP) on health care, Canada 9.3 per cent and Honduras 8.6 per cent. However, poorer countries such as Belize, Nicaragua and Guatemala cannot afford to invest such a large proportion of their GDP – typically the figure is between 2 and 3 per cent for them.

The proportion of people with access to clean water varies from almost 100 per cent in the United States, Canada and Barbados, to 77 per cent in Nicaragua and 46 per cent in Haiti. Particular problem areas include shanty towns and rural areas. For example, in Mexico 95 per cent of urban residents have access to clean water, but only 69 per cent of rural people do.

Closely linked to water is the issue of sanitation. In Barbados, Canada and the United States 100 per cent of the population has access to adequate sanitation. This proportion falls to 74 per cent in Mexico, 50 per cent in Belize and 28 per cent in Haiti. In Haiti, 50 per cent of the urban population benefits from adequate sanitation, but only 16 per cent of rural people. In contrast, in Cuba where there has been much greater government investment in health and welfare, 99 per cent of the urban population and 95 per cent of the rural population have access to sanitation.

Not everyone has private access to clean water. This man is using public washing facilities in a street in Cozumel, Mexico.

URBAN VERSUS RURAL

Many of the smaller countries in North America are still largely rural, while the more developed countries have higher levels of urbanization (the proportion of people living in urban areas). Nevertheless, some Caribbean islands have very high rates of urbanization (a measure of how quickly the proportion in urban areas is increasing). Across Central America and the Caribbean the proportion of people living in urban areas ranges from 40 per cent in Guatemala to over 95 per cent in Puerto Rico and Guadeloupe. In general, the proportion of people living in urban areas is increasing

FACT FILE

In New York, the daily average water consumption is 448 litres (98 gallons) per person, in Cuidad Juarez, Mexico, it is 336 litres (74 gallons) per person, while in Havana, Cuba, it is just 100 litres (22 gallons) per person.

rapidly. In 1940, only 35 per cent of Mexico's population lived in urban areas. By 2001 it was 74.6 per cent.

Rural communities in North America range from small, isolated communities in Nunavut, Canada (see page 11), to densely populated lowlands on Caribbean islands such as Antigua. Most rural communities were traditionally associated with farming, but many are now becoming involved in services, including tourism, with residents commuting to nearby urban areas for work. The decline in farm work is partly due to increased use of machinery in farming, meaning there is less demand for labour, but is also a result of the low wages traditionally paid to farm workers.

About 75 per cent of the US population lives in cities and large towns. Many cities are so large that they have grown together with neighbouring suburbs to form large metropolitan areas. New York is a good example of such an area. The city itself is made up of five boroughs – Brooklyn, the Bronx, Manhattan, Staten Island and Queens – each of which is also a county of New York state. The New York metropolitan area includes numerous cities and towns in neighbouring Long Island and

FACT FILE

Since 1970, levels of urbanization have increased rapidly in Honduras, from 29 per cent in 1970 to 45.6 per cent in 2003.

A busy Fifth Avenue in New York City. The northeast United States is an area of very high population density.

other parts of New York state, and even parts of New Jersey and Connecticut. Some multiple metropolitan areas with economic and transportation links, or those that have physically grown together, are considered one megalopolis, or densely populated region, even across state lines.

URBAN DEVELOPMENT

Urban development has reached massive proportions in parts of North America. A consequence of this growth has been that large cities such as Mexico City and Los Angeles now have major problems with traffic congestion and the related pollution from vehicle emissions. Population growth in smaller urban areas is also significant. Between 1975 and 2000, for example, the population of the metropolitan area of Phoenix, Arizona, grew by over 2 million people to 3.23 million. The expansion of Phoenix is due to a number of factors including a diverse economy, pleasant climate, good quality of life and relatively low cost of living – all of which have encouraged companies to relocate there. Such rapid growth leads to suburban sprawl, as cities expand rapidly around their edges to accommodate the influx of people.

The quality of life in urban areas is highly variable. In general, high-quality lifestyles in suburban areas contrast with the deprivation of ghettos and shanty towns in less developed parts of North America. Even in small cities, such as Castries in St Lucia, there is visible evidence of inequalities in standards of living. In the larger urban areas, hot spots of deprivation are to be found in inner cities such as Watts in central Los Angeles, as well as in shanty towns such as Naucalpan, Ecatepec and Netzahualcoyotl on the edge of Mexico City.

FACT FILE

One-fifth of the US population lives on just one-fiftieth of the land area of the country, in the area from Boston to Washington.

The rural, hillside community of San Mateo, in Guatemala.

4. RELIGION AND CULTURE IN NORTH AMERICA

MANY PEOPLE IN NORTH AMERICA HAVE STRONG RELIGIOUS BELIEFS. For many of the early European migrants, and for other immigrants to North America, the promise of religious tolerance – particularly in the United States – was especially attractive.

FACT FILE

Some 97 per cent of the Christian population in Central America, 47 per cent of Canadian Christians and 21 per cent of Christians in the United States are Roman Catholic.

RELIGION IN NORTH AMERICA

In the United States today over 60 per cent of people are Christian, and some 40 per cent attend religious services regularly. There are 60 million Roman Catholics and 100 million Protestants in the United States. Protestant religions include a number of denominations, such as Baptists, Lutherans, the Society of Friends (Quakers), Amish and Adventists. Other important religious groups include Jews (6 million), Muslims (6 million), Hindus and Buddhists. Two of the fastest-growing religious groups in the United States are the Mormons (the Church of Jesus Christ of Latter-day Saints) and the Christian Scientists (the Church of Christ, Scientist).

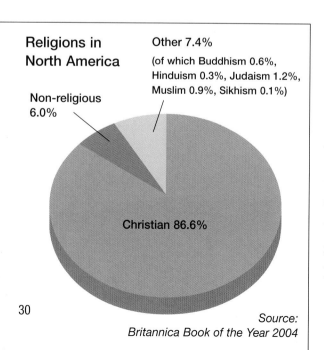

Religions in North America

Other 7.4%
(of which Buddhism 0.6%, Hinduism 0.3%, Judaism 1.2%, Muslim 0.9%, Sikhism 0.1%)

Non-religious 6.0%

Christian 86.6%

Source: Britannica Book of the Year 2004

Large numbers of people with the same religious faith live in some areas of the United States. For example, members of the Mormon Church account for 77 per cent of the population in Utah and 27 per cent in Idaho. The Mormons settled in Utah in the 19th century to escape from the opposition to their beliefs that they encountered elsewhere. The so-called 'Bible-belt' – an area of traditional Protestant worshippers in the United States – stretches from Virginia to Texas and Missouri. Baptists form the majority of the

Christian population in Mississippi, Alabama and Georgia. Roman Catholics are associated with areas of Irish immigration, such as the northern cities of New York, Boston and Chicago, and more recently with Latino immigration, for example in southern Florida and California. On a much smaller scale, the Amish are associated with Pennsylvania.

The Roman Catholic Church, United Church of Canada and Anglican churches have the largest following in Canada. Over 75 per cent of Jews in Canada live in Toronto and Montreal, while members of the Presbyterian Church are centred in Ontario, and Canadian Baptists live primarily in the Maritime Provinces of the east coast. Roman Catholicism is centred around areas of French immigration, such as Québec.

Most of the countries of Central America are predominantly Roman Catholic. The Spanish *conquistadors* (see page 8) first brought Catholicism to the region, closely followed by missionaries who worked to convert the Native Americans to their religion. Belize, which came under British rather than Spanish influence, has been mainly Protestant, although the proportion of Catholics in Belize is increasing. Much of the black population along the Caribbean coast is Protestant, also a result of British colonialism. In the Caribbean there are many supporters of Rastafarianism. Rastafarians believe that Haile Selassie, the former Emperor of Ethiopia, was the Messiah, and that all believers will some day return to Ethiopia.

FACT FILE

In parts of the Caribbean, notably Haiti, over half of the population practise voodoo, a combination of Roman Catholicism and West African beliefs and rituals.

A Christian Holy Week procession in Guatemala.

POR QUE BUSCAN ENTRE LOS MUERTOS

Two men from Chichimila in Yucatán (Mexico) cook sacred foods during a rain ceremony.

The Green Bay Packers play the Washington Redskins in a National Football League game.

Some traditional Native American beliefs still persist in North America. In the past, many Inuits were converted to Christianity and their own religions were forbidden. Today some have returned to their ancient practices and beliefs. Similarly, in parts of Central America indigenous populations such as the Maya continue to hold traditional beliefs, for example worship of the Rain God. Some islanders in the eastern Caribbean believe in *obeah*, a type of black magic used to cast spells on an enemy. *Obeah* uses magical rituals to reach supernatural forces.

SPORT

The United States is particularly known for baseball, basketball and American Rules Football. The game of baseball originated from the English game, rounders. The World Series was first held in 1903 between the winners of the two professional leagues in the United States, now known as the National League and the American League. American Rules Football is probably the most popular spectator sport, with 90 million people watching the Super Bowl Championship alone. In Canada, popular winter sports include skiing, skating and ice hockey – which was invented in Montreal in 1835. A Native American game called 'baggatway' was developed in Canada into lacrosse. In addition, many Canadian teams, such as the Toronto Blue Jays, play baseball in the US-based major leagues.

Football (soccer) is the most popular sport in Mexico, and indeed throughout Central America. Mexico hosted the 1970 Football World Cup, as did the United States in 1994. Basketball also has a big

following in Mexico, as well as other sports that are Spanish in origin such as bull-fighting, rodeo and *jai alai. Jai alai* is a fast ball game, based on the Spanish game *pelota*, in which two, four or six players use long, curved wicker baskets to hit a ball – the *pelota* – inside a walled court.

In parts of the Caribbean, cricket is extremely popular. It was introduced to the region by British colonists, and is a bat-and-ball game played between two teams of eleven players. The West Indies cricket team is made up of players from all over the Caribbean, and the Test Matches (games against other countries) are played on cricket pitches (grounds) in Trinidad, Antigua, St Lucia, Barbados and Jamaica. Famous cricketers include Sir Garfield (Gary) Sobers and Brian Lara.

Recreational water sports are also important, especially in the Caribbean and along the coastlines and lakes of the United States. Sailing, windsurfing, scuba diving and swimming are popular among tourists as well as local people.

North America has produced many world-class, Olympic athletes including Carl Lewis (a sprinter and long-jump athlete who won nine gold medals in four Olympic Games) and Mark Spitz (who won a record seven gold medals for swimming in the 1972 Munich Olympics). Famous Jamaican sprinters include Marlene Ottey and Lennox Miller. During the 1990s, Cubans such as Felix Savon dominated Olympic boxing. Donovan Bailey, a Canadian track star, is one of the many sports personalities who has made a successful transition from the sports field into sports management.

Informal games of cricket are a very familiar sight in the Caribbean.

FACT FILE

In terms of employment, the sports industry in the United States is larger than the film, radio, television and education services combined. It accounts for over 2.3 million jobs and US$48 billion in wages and salaries.

FACT FILE

At the 2004 Olympics in Athens, the United States won thirty-five gold medals, Cuba nine, Canada three and the Bahamas one.

The most famous of all reggae singers was Bob Marley, seen here in performance in 1980. Reggae musicians often sing about social conditions because their music developed as a form of protest against the various discriminations they faced.

MUSIC

The Caribbean has a very rich musical heritage, with roots in Africa, Spain, France, England and Ireland. Calypso originated in the 18th century in Trinidad as satirical songs sung in French by slaves working on the plantations. Modern calypso has sharp political and social messages. Well known calypso artists include the Mighty Sparrow, David Rudder and Winston 'Gypsy' Peters. Similarly, blues music in the United States grew from the songs that slaves sang on plantations. Blues was very important in the development of jazz and had a huge influence on popular music and rock 'n' roll during the 20th century in the United States.

Ska evolved in Jamaica in the 1950s. It is a blend of calypso, rhythm and blues, and African-Jamaican folk music. Similarly, reggae is a blend of ska, blues, calypso and rock. Many of the songs are borne out of social protest, and were popularized by the late Bob Marley. In contrast, zonk originated in the French West Indies and is a mix of African and French dance music.

A TV CONTINENT

There are over one thousand television stations in North America, although most are local channels that are usually affiliates (smaller associates) of larger broadcast networks. Americans have more choices in their television viewing than anyone else in the world. Many channels – particularly cable channels – are dedicated to providing a single type of programming, such as sport, education or news, movies or entertainment. Many programmes, such as *Friends* or *The Simpsons*, have become popular worldwide.

THE CAR

The car is an integral part of North American culture. The United States has more cars per person than any other country in North America – 481 cars per thousand people (ranked 12th in the world), whereas Haiti has the lowest ratio at 4.4 cars per thousand people. Within the United States, up to 90 per cent of journeys made between towns and cities are taken in cars. Increased ownership of cars has allowed cities to spread out – a process known as urban sprawl. The trend towards bigger 'gas-guzzling' sports utility vehicles (SUVs) in recent years is a serious environmental issue in the United States. In Mexico City there are some 3.5 million vehicles, producing some of the most polluted air in the world.

FOOD

Fast food is another feature of North American culture, mainly in the United States but also in Canada and increasingly in Mexico. While fast food has contributed to the rise in obesity in the United States and in Mexico, other factors such as increasingly sedentary lifestyles, changes in diet and large food-portion sizes are also blamed for this trend. Thanks to the many different ethnic groups who have settled in the United States, for example Italian, Mexican and Chinese, a wide variety of food is available in restaurants in even the smallest towns across the country. The United States is also a country of meat-eaters – particularly beef.

Detroit, Michigan, is one of the most important regions of car manufacturing in the world and hosting the International Motor Show (above) is good for sales of new cars.

FACT FILE

Up to seven million new vehicles are bought every year in the United States.

FACT FILE

The United States has the longest road network in the world – 6,304,193 km (3,917,425 miles).

5. NATURAL RESOURCES IN NORTH AMERICA

NORTH AMERICA, IN PARTICULAR THE UNITED STATES, is a continent rich in natural resources.

OIL AND NATURAL GAS

In the United States, oil and natural gas are found in Alaska, the Gulf States of Texas and Louisiana, Oklahoma, California, Pennsylvania and Kentucky. In Canada, oil and gas reserves in Alberta supply 50 per cent of the country's oil and 90 per cent of its natural gas requirements.

Mexico is one of the largest oil-exporting nations outside OPEC (Organization of Petroleum Exporting Countries – made up mainly of the oil-producing countries in the Middle East). In 2003 Mexico achieved an output of 3.8 million barrels of oil per day (the main OPEC countries produce 24 million barrels of oil per day). Most of the production comes from the Gulf of Mexico. Trinidad also exports natural gas and oil, mainly to the United States, and has major petrochemical industries.

COAL

There are huge reserves of coal in the western United States. Most of the coal mining is done by opencast mining in which the surface layer is removed and the exposed coal then mined. However, this type of mining has a dramatic effect on the

FACT FILE

In 2003, Alaska's 2,486 oil wells produced 355.6 million barrels of oil, about 22 per cent of US oil production for that year.

A quarry in Pennsylvania. The environmental effects of opencast mining are serious as well as visually unattractive.

Energy planners are keen to develop the vast oil resources that exist in Alaska. Alaskan oil provides nearly one-third of the total oil reserves in the United States and one-eighth of its total natural gas reserves. Those in favour of development claim that most Alaskans see oil as their main source of jobs and wealth in the future.

However, some Native American groups claim they would prefer to live in their traditional way rather than benefit from oil income. In northern Alaska, the seven thousand people of the Gwich'in Nation

consider the coastal plain of the Arctic Refuge sacred because it is the calving ground for the porcupine caribou herd. The subsistence lifestyle of the Gwich'in is intimately bound to this herd for food, clothing and tools made from caribou antlers and bone. As a result, the Gwich'in vigorously oppose any oil development in the region.

Part of the operation to clean up the oil from the tanker the *Exxon Valdez* after it ran aground in Prince William Sound, Alaska, in 1989. About 42 million litres (11 million gallons) of spilt oil polluted 2,100 km (1,200 miles) of the Alaskan shoreline.

environment by removing natural vegetation, reducing biodiversity and ruining the landscape. For example, in West Virginia, opencast mining at Pigeonroost Hollow has destroyed much of the natural forest and wildlife. There are important coal reserves in Canada too – a large proportion of the mined reserves in British Columbia are exported to Japan. Fossil fuels account for over 75 per cent of Mexico's energy production.

FACT FILE

The United States has 500 billion tonnes (492 billion tons) of coal – enough to last three hundred years.

Hydroelectric power on the Kootenay River, British Columbia, Canada. HEP has great potential in many parts of North America.

FACT FILE

Hydroelectric power (HEP) accounts for over 80 per cent of electricity production in Costa Rica, 52 per cent in Guatemala, 50 per cent in Honduras, and 30 per cent in El Salvador.

HYDROELECTRIC POWER

Hydroelectric power (HEP) is very important in Canada. It accounts for nearly 66 per cent of the country's electricity generation and 97 per cent of its renewable electricity generation. The largest HEP plant in Canada is located at James Bay in Québec. Canada exports electricity to the United States, as well as crude petroleum and natural gas. HEP supplies almost 15 per cent of Mexico's electricity production. The mountainous landscapes of Central America have many narrow, steep valleys which are relatively easy to dam. Combined with high rainfall and high water levels, these dams provide a plentiful supply of HEP for the Central American countries.

RENEWABLE ENERGY

There are a number of examples of projects making use of other forms of renewable energy apart from HEP. In Belize, for example, electricity is generated by burning biomass (biodegradable material such as sawdust), and solar power is used to generate electricity and heat water in health clinics. In Honduras, biomass (sugar cane waste pulp) is also used for the generation of electricity at Tres Valles. Nicaragua uses solar energy for health clinics, while Panama has developed a solar water-pumping system for farms as well as using solar power in its national parks to provide energy in research stations and tourist camps.

Both the United States and Mexico have considerable potential for geothermal energy – tapping heat from the interior of the earth to produce energy. However, there has been a decline in the production of geothermal energy in the United States in recent years, due to the overexploitation of the giant Geysers steam field in California. As water is taken out of the geyser reservoir, the pressure in the reservoir drops, making it more difficult and costly to extract water and causing a gradual decline in levels of productivity. In Mexico, Costa Rica, El Salvador and Guatemala money is being invested in geothermal energy, and there has been a substantial increase in capacity in recent years.

The Honduran government has brought solar energy to many remote and isolated towns, such as here at San Ramon Centro, where solar energy powers the school's computer centre.

MINERALS

Mineral resources are widespread throughout the continent. Canada is the world's leading producer of nickel, zinc, uranium and potash. It is also a major producer of cobalt, gypsum and asbestos. Mexico is the world's leading producer of silver. In some countries, such as Haiti, there are mineral resources including gold, copper and bauxite that are not mined, mainly as a result of the political upheavals of the last forty years. Jamaica has large reserves of bauxite, which is the raw material used to produce aluminium. In the 1970s, production was mostly controlled by foreign companies, but more recently the government has imposed a levy (tax) on bauxite production so that more of the benefits will return directly to Jamaica.

FACT FILE

Trinidad is the most resource-rich island in the Caribbean, with oil, asphalt and natural gas. Fossil fuels account for 99.8 per cent of its energy production.

FORESTRY

There are important timber resources in the Rockies, the Pacific Northwest (Oregon and Washington) and in Alaska. Forests cover over 40 per cent of Canada and about half of them are

Forestry is an important part of the economy in large parts of Canada.

commercially operated. Most of the trees cut in Canada are softwood, coniferous trees. Canada is the world's largest producer of newspaper, the second largest producer of pulp and the third largest producer of sawn timber. Forestry is also important in Central America. However, in some places deforestation has become a major problem. Many of the rainforests of Central America have been cut down to make space for farmland. In Panama, large-scale deforestation is leading to serious soil erosion which in turn is causing the Panama Canal to silt up. If this problem is not addressed, the movement of ships through the canal between the Atlantic and Pacific oceans could be affected.

FARMING

North America is ranked third behind Asia and Europe in farming production. It produces approximately 60 per cent of the world's soybeans and 50 per cent of the world's maize and sorghum. It also produces about 25 per cent of the world's citrus fruits and oats.

Farming benefits from the deep, fertile, black earth in the Midwestern United States, while the Great Plains of Canada and the United States are major wheat-growing regions. In the drier western and southwestern regions, irrigation is used to produce alfalfa, cotton and sugar. Wheat, beans and maize are important crops grown in Mexico, while in tropical parts of Central America and the Caribbean, coffee and bananas are vital crops.

The rich soils in Central America support a thriving farming system. However, the mountainous terrain limits production in many areas, although terraces – artificial steps cut into the steep slopes – are used to grow crops in places such as Montserrat and St Lucia. Farming accounts for a large percentage of exports in these countries. For example, in 2002 exports of bananas and sugar were worth nearly US$3 billion for the economy of Guatemala and nearly US$1.3 billion for Honduras.

FISHING

About 25 per cent of the world's annual fish catch comes from the North Atlantic Ocean between Newfoundland and New England. The Gulf of Mexico is important for menhaden (used for fertilizer and fishmeal), shrimp and lobsters. The main species caught in the Bering Sea, the Gulf of Alaska, and the Northern Pacific include pollock, sardines, mackerel and anchovies. Salmon is an important catch in the Pacific waters of Canada and Alaska. However, over-fishing has reduced stocks in British Columbia, Alaska and Washington state. In British Columbia, salmon are now raised in fish farms. Likewise, the cod fisheries in the Atlantic Ocean have nearly disappeared. As a result, both the Canadian and US governments have placed restrictions on fishing in some of their waters.

FACT FILE

Up to 80 per cent of commercially valuable fish populations in US fisheries are already fully exploited or over-exploited.

FACT FILE

In 1992 Canada's cod industry collapsed due to over-fishing, leading to the loss of forty thousand jobs. It remains perilous despite a C$3.9 billion Fisheries and Adjustment Plan to revitalize the fishing industry.

Catching salmon off the Alaskan coast. Fishing remains an important source of employment and income for many coastal and river communities.

6. THE NORTH AMERICAN ECONOMY

*T*HE ECONOMY OF NORTH AMERICA IS THE THIRD LARGEST IN the world behind Europe and Asia. It continues to expand, and grew by over 2 per cent in 2002. It benefits from a vast array of natural resources as well as a large and wealthy market. It also has a strong high-tech base, including research and development.

FACT FILE

The United States has the world's largest industrial output, worth US$2,684 billion in 2003. Canada was ninth, with an industrial output worth US$190 billion.

Silicon Valley – the home of high-technology industry in California.

THE UNITED STATES

The US economy is a market-oriented economy, which means that private individuals and business firms make most of the decisions. Many of these companies are extremely large and have dealings with suppliers and customers around the world. Large numbers of multinational companies were founded and have their headquarters in the United States, including Microsoft, Ford and General Motors.

There are two main contrasting economic zones within the United States. The 'rust belt' refers to the older, industrial regions of northeast and north central United States, which were based around manufacturing jobs, coal, iron and steel. The 'sunbelt' refers to areas from Florida in the east to California in the west which have attracted industries that do not need to be located close to a raw material, including electronics and software companies such as Dell Computers in Texas and Motorola in Phoenix. Many high-tech companies are located in California's so-called 'Silicon Valley', about 80 km (50 miles) south of

San Francisco. Other high-tech industries are found elsewhere. For example, the Microsoft Corporation is based in Seattle.

Many US companies have moved jobs out of the United States to benefit from cheap foreign labour and advantageous taxes. Examples include call-centres in Jamaica, the *maquiladoras* (industries that pay very low wages to produce goods cheaply) in Mexico, and Operation Bootstrap in Puerto Rico –

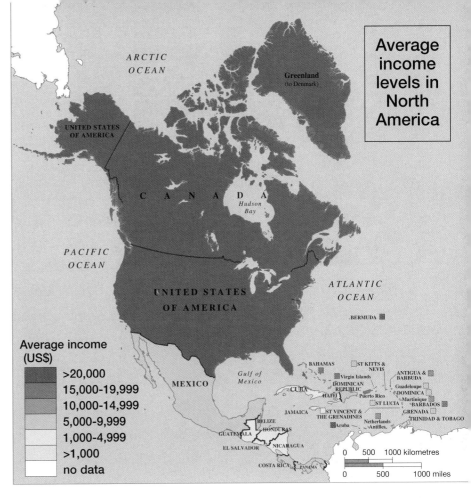

a program of governmental support for industry through tax breaks. However, much of this outsourcing has gone to Asia, where the Indian software industry has taken over work that was formerly carried out in the United States.

CANADA

Canada is an affluent, high-tech, industrial society. Since World War II, Canada has been transformed from a largely rural economy into one that is primarily industrial and urban. Both the 1989 US-Canada Free Trade Agreement (FTA), and the 1994 North American Free Trade Agreement (NAFTA) between the United States, Canada and Mexico, led to a huge increase in trade and economic integration with the United States. However, Canada does face one major problem – the southward migration to the United States of professionals lured by the prospect of higher pay and lower taxes.

FACT FILE

With worldwide sales of over $237.1 billion, the US company ExxonMobil is ranked second among the world's largest companies. Its sales are greater than the GDP of Sweden or Turkey!

Many low-paid jobs have moved from the United States to other parts of North America, such as those found in the *maquiladoras* industries on the US-Mexico border.

FACT FILE

In Mexico, industry accounts for 25 per cent of employment and 18 per cent of Mexico's GDP.

MEXICO

Although Mexico has substantial energy and mineral resources, it has not fully developed its economy. Population growth is faster than the growth of jobs, and the agricultural sector is weak. Most of the manufacturing in Mexico occurs in and around Mexico City and along the US-Mexican border in assembly factories (*maquiladoras*). Income distribution remains highly unbalanced – the richest 10 per cent of households receive 41 per cent of the national income, and the poorest 10 per cent of all households receive just 1.6 per cent.

TRADE AGREEMENTS

There have been a number of agreements between the various countries of North America to open up each other's markets. The North American Free Trade Agreement (NAFTA) between Mexico, Canada and the United States allows free trade between the three countries. Mexico's trade with the United States and Canada has tripled since the implementation of NAFTA in 1994. Mexico has also made free-trade agreements with Guatemala, Honduras, El Salvador, and the European Free Trade Association (Iceland, Norway, Switzerland and Liechtenstein), putting more than 90 per cent of Mexico's trade under such agreements. Some people argue that NAFTA allows US companies to exploit cheap labour in Mexico, as well as giving them increased access to new markets. Others say that thousands of high-paying manufacturing jobs have been lost in the United States because lower labour costs in Mexico have led companies to move jobs south of the border.

In 2004 the United States, Costa Rica, El Salvador, Guatemala, Honduras and Nicaragua signed the Central American Free Trade Agreement (CAFTA). Under CAFTA, tariffs have been removed to increase the amount of trade between the United States and the Central American countries. Critics of CAFTA argue that the agreement could make poverty worse in Central America, because it allows the export of staple products such as rice, maize and beans from the United States. These crops are heavily subsidized in the United States, and because farmers in other CAFTA countries may be unable to compete with the low prices, their livelihoods may be threatened as a result.

The Central America Common Market (CACM) was established in 1961 by El Salvador, Guatemala, Honduras and Nicaragua. Costa Rica joined in 1962. The aim of CACM is to foster economic development and co-operation between the smaller countries of Central America and to attract industrial investment. Despite problems due to political instability in some countries, CACM has been reasonably successful at lowering trade barriers between its member countries.

HONDURAS

Honduras is one of the poorest countries in the Western hemisphere with an extraordinarily unequal distribution of income. It is hoping for expanded trade opportunities under the Enhanced Caribbean Basin Initiative to improve trade and economic opportunities, and for aid as part of the Heavily Indebted Poor Countries (HIPC) initiative (see page 46). But growth remains dependent on the status of the US economy, Honduras' major trading partner, on prices of major commodities such as coffee, and on the reduction of the high crime rate.

FACT FILE

In Honduras, the richest 10 per cent of households receive 43 per cent of the country's income, while the poorest 10 per cent receive only 0.6 per cent. Over 40 per cent of the population survives on less than US$2 per day.

Washing bananas at a plantation in San Pedro Sula, Honduras. Many jobs in farming are low-paid and unskilled.

43

FACT FILE

Nicaragua's debt repayments rose from 2.3 per cent of the value of its exports in 1990 to 22.2 per cent in 2001.

DEBT

There is widespread debt in North America. Debt repayments (as a percentage of exports of goods and services) are as high as 24.5 per cent in Belize and 22.2 per cent in Nicaragua. In practical terms, this 'debt burden' means that a poor country may be paying out more in debt service (interest) payments than it can afford to spend on vital services such as health and education. Nevertheless, in the 1990s Mexico managed to reduce its debt burden from 18.3 per cent to 14.1 per cent, while Jamaica's debt burden has come down from 27 per cent to 16.8 per cent. Many of the Caribbean islands, such as the Dominican Republic, Grenada, Haiti, St Vincent and Trinidad and Tobago, have a debt burden of below 10 per cent. Some countries with great poverty and high debt burdens, such as Honduras and Nicaragua, are receiving aid under a scheme run by the World Bank – the Heavily Indebted Poor Countries scheme. This scheme aims to provide debt relief in return for sound economic policies and measures for reducing poverty.

THE CARIBBEAN

The Caribbean Community and Common Market (CARICOM) was established in 1973 to promote economic development across the Caribbean. CARICOM also makes policies covering a wide range of issues from health to the environment. Nevertheless, the economies of many of the Caribbean islands remain vulnerable. Many are highly dependent on tourism for income, for example the Bahamas, Barbados and St Lucia all earn more than one-third of their GDP from tourism. In Antigua tourism accounts for more than half of GDP, and low tourist numbers since early 2000 have slowed its economy.

Despite its reliance on tourism, the economy of St Lucia is one of the more

Harvesting sugar cane in Barbados. Farming has been mechanized in many of the Caribbean countries.

stable in the Caribbean. St Lucia has been able to attract foreign business and investment, especially in its offshore banking and tourism industries. Its manufacturing sector is the most diverse in the eastern Caribbean area, and the St Lucia government is trying to revitalize the banana industry. St Lucia's manufacturing base is varied, including plastics and textiles, coconut products, cigarettes, rum, mineral water, toys, cardboard cartons and electronic components.

Similarly, the economy of Barbados has been dependent on sugar cane cultivation and related activities, but in recent years it has diversified into manufacturing and tourism. Today, 15 per cent of the workforce is employed in manufacturing and 75 per cent in services, including tourism, offshore finance and information services.

FACT FILE

In 2004, the Caribbean region attracted 22 million tourists, the United States 50.89 million and Mexico 20.64 million.

• • • • • • ▶ IN FOCUS: Small Island Economies

Small island economies face a number of issues. Their size means there is a small home market (Dominica's population is just 79,000; that of Barbados is 270,000). There is also a limited variety of natural resources and often a shortage of skilled labour. Many islands are remote, such as Barbados or Montserrat, and this leads to increased transport costs. In the Caribbean there is the additional problem of hurricanes. Nevertheless, being surrounded by water and having a tropical climate provide the ideal conditions for coastal tourism. The insularity encouraged by island-living may also strengthen cultural and social identities, for example the calypso and reggae (see page 34) associated with places such as Jamaica and Trinidad.

Tourists visit the Caribbean for its 'winter sun', beautiful beaches and clear seas.

47

7. NORTH AMERICA IN THE WORLD

NORTH AMERICA IS AN IMPORTANT GLOBAL REGION IN BOTH **economic and political terms. The United States in particular has a vital role as the world's only superpower, following the collapse of the Soviet Union in 1991.**

THE UNITED STATES

Even before it became the only superpower, the United States took a lead role in global affairs. After the end of World War II, it helped to rebuild a war-devastated Europe and to oversee the foundation of major global institutions such as the United Nations (UN), the World Bank and the International Monetary Fund. These institutions all have their headquarters in the United States today. Another key role for the United States has been as a global mediator in regions of conflict such as the former Yugoslavia and Israel – indeed it has a long history of attempting to bring about peace agreements between Israel and its Arab neighbours. When Iraq invaded Kuwait in 1991, however, the United States and its allies responded with the Gulf War. This role as 'global policeman' has continued in the 21st century, with the United States leading a war in Iraq in 2003.

A US soldier speaks to an Iraqi voter during the elections held in January 2005. In many places, people queued for hours in order to vote.

Since the terrorist attacks of 11 September 2001 (9/11), the United States has collaborated with other North American and worldwide partners in the fight against terrorist activities. Under President George W. Bush, the United States led the search for Osama bin Laden and the fight against Al-Qaeda (the organization behind the 9/11 attacks), the attack on Afghanistan (the country in which bin Laden was believed to be living), and the defeat of the Taliban regime (the political leaders of Afghanistan). In 2003, US troops overthrew the regime of the Iraqi dictator, Saddam Hussein. Since that time largely US and British peace-keeping forces have tried to control the escalating violence in Iraq. Democratic elections for a new Iraqi government took place in January 2005.

North America compared with the rest of the world

Population	
Land area	
Economy	

Percentage of global total

Source: United Nations; World Bank; Britannica Book of the Year 2004

CANADA

Canada's most important international relationship in terms of trade is with the United States (77 per cent of exports and 65 per cent of imports). However, there are a number of disagreements between the two countries, such as disputes about the levels of pollution given off by US businesses close to the Canadian border. Traditionally the main focus of trade for Canada was with Western Europe, but today most of Canada's trade is with Pacific Rim countries (including the United States), where there are new markets emerging and fast economic growth.

FACT FILE

Canada gives more than twice as much government aid to foreign countries in relation to GDP as the United States: 0.25 per cent of GDP compared with 0.1 per cent in the United States.

In recent years, the focus of Canadian aid has switched from West Africa to southeast Asia and eastern European countries, with particular emphasis on health, education and child protection. Canadian troops have also been involved in recent United Nations (UN) peacekeeping operations, including those in Afghanistan, Somalia and the former Yugoslavia.

A Canadian soldier patrols the streets of Mitrovicia, Kosovo, in 2000.

MEXICO

Mexico's main trading relationship is with the United States, and the signing of NAFTA (see pages 43-4) has increased this role. Mexico's close ties with its northern neighbour, and the processes of modernization and development put in place by its government, have resulted in its having less in common with its poorer neighbours to the south. Nevertheless, Mexico has played an important role mediating conflicts in El Salvador, Guatemala and Nicaragua.

PANAMA

Panama is another country that is trying to balance its relationship with the United States and its credibility with its neighbours. Panama received US$8.3 million in aid from the United States in 2004 and is expected to enter a free trade arrangement with the United States shortly. Ever since the construction of the Panama Canal, the United States has been involved in Panama's internal affairs. During the 1980s, an army general named Manuel Noriega became very influential in Panama. After a disputed election in 1989, Noriega seized power in Panama, declaring himself Head of State. US president George H.W. Bush sent troops into Panama to overthrow Noriega, who eventually surrendered. Noriega was imprisoned in the United States for drug trafficking offences. Since that time, Panama has had a succession of civilian governments, and in 1999 the United States handed over control of the Panama Canal to Panama for the first time since its construction.

FACT FILE

The Panama Canal, opened in 1914, is crucial to trade in the region. It saves a massive 4,800 km (3,000 miles) off the journey from the eastern seaboard of the United States to its Pacific coast.

Manuel Noriega with supporters in Panama City in 1989, before his arrest by US forces.

CARIBBEAN

Most Caribbean countries retain strong ties with their former colonial powers. Antigua and St Lucia, for example, have close economic, social and political ties with the UK. Many Caribbean countries have trade deals with the European Union to provide agricultural products, such as bananas. The United States has complained about this arrangement, claiming that it is a violation of free trade and is unfair to the operations of US companies in Central America, since they do not have the same preferential access to the European Union market.

CUBA

For much of the 20th century, Cuba's main trading partner was the United States. By the 1950s approximately 65 per cent of Cuba's exports and 75 per cent of its imports were with the United States. However, following the revolution that brought Fidel Castro to power (see page 13), Cuba's trade shifted to the former Soviet Union and the Communist countries of eastern Europe. When Communism collapsed in eastern Europe and the Soviet Union, Cuba was forced to seek new trading partners. With US sanctions still in place today, Cuba trades mainly with Canada, China, the Netherlands, Russia and Spain. Sugar remains the prime export, although nickel, citrus fruits, coffee and tobacco are also exported. Tourism is increasingly important, with over five million visitors a year to Cuba anticipated by 2010.

Street entertainment in the capital of Cuba, Havana, as a musical group play traditional Cuban music outside Havana Cathedral. Tourism is the great economic hope for many countries in North America.

8. WILDLIFE IN NORTH AMERICA

NORTH AMERICA HAS MANY FAMOUS ANIMALS SUCH AS **alligators, bald eagles, bison (buffalo), caribou, grizzly bears and** cougars as well as species specific to tropical areas such as manatees and leatherback turtles.

Caribou are just one of the many migratory species that travel vast distances to reach their summer grazing in Alaska.

THE FAR NORTH

In the Arctic and coniferous forests of northern Canada and Alaska there are caribou and wolves. Caribou are migratory and move northwards in the summer to feast on the tundra vegetation. The deciduous forests of northeastern North America are home to a wide variety of mammals, including bears, deer, skunks and squirrels. The twenty to thirty species of trees in these forests support a huge variety of insects (over three hundred species of insects can live on an oak tree), offering a wide range of food supply for a large variety of mammals. In contrast, the trees of the northern coniferous forests support only one to two species per hectare of trees. In turn, a restricted food supply means there is less variety of bird life and mammals. Typical species in these forests include moose, beavers and timber wolves.

THE DRY LANDS

Deserts are normally considered to be barren areas, but in North America they offer habitats to more than one hundred species of birds and over forty species of mammals. Desert birds include the roadrunner and the burrowing owl, which lives in the abandoned burrows of prairie dogs. Small mammals include the ground squirrel and kangaroo rat, and there are also mountain lions, rattlesnakes and coyotes. Most desert mammals are very efficient in their use of water, and generally extract adequate moisture from their main food source.

GRASSLANDS

The grasslands of the Great Plains of the United States and Canada were once dominated by large numbers of just a few species of mammals. The Great Plains were home to vast numbers of bison and pronghorn antelope. The bison were brought to the edge of extinction in the mid- to late-19th century. Where once there were thirty to sixty million bison there are now between 250,000 and 350,000, mostly in private herds in protected areas. Smaller mammals include the prairie dog, which lives in underground colonies that normally contain hundreds of individual animals at densities of up 600 per sq km (1,550 per sq mile). Predators of the prairie dog include the coyote, the prairie falcon and the burrowing owl.

ENDANGERED HABITATS

Some wildlife habitats are disappearing fast, largely due to urbanization and farming. For example, only 10 per cent of North America's prairies remain as grassland – 71 per cent have been converted to cropland and 19 per cent

FACT FILE

Kangaroo rats are the most common of the mammals in North America's deserts. They are physically adapted to survive heat and drought, and are even found in California's Death Valley.

FACT FILE

When the thawing of snow or heavy rain floods the plains, prairie dogs raise small mounds at the entrances to their tunnels to prevent water getting in. In some cases they build tunnels vertically so that they can survive in air pockets.

Prairie dogs are very social animals.

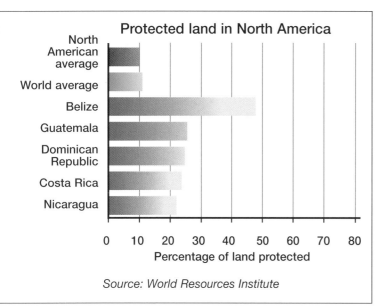

Protected land in North America

Percentage of land protected

Source: World Resources Institute

have been settled. Other developments, such as tourism and leisure-related constructions, are having negative impacts on vulnerable coastal, wetland and mountainous areas. On many of the Caribbean islands, building for the tourist industry has had a detrimental effect on the environment. For example, at Rodney Bay in St Lucia, natural vegetation has been cut away to make space for the construction of hotels and marinas.

The Florida Everglades is a unique wetland that supports a variety of reptiles, including alligators; amphibians; and wading birds such as flamingos and herons. Just under half (47 per cent) of the area is protected as a national park. However, large-scale drainage programs have reduced the volume of water reaching the Everglades, while fertilizers and pesticides have contaminated some of the water that flows into the region.

The Everglades in Florida is home to many semi-aquatic species of reptile, such as this alligator.

FACT FILE

The Florida panther is highly endangered. In the 1990s, closely related panthers from Texas were brought to Florida, and there has since been successful breeding in captivity. Increased protection of the environment may yet save the species.

FACT FILE

Most of Mexico's tropical rainforest has been destroyed. Only about 5 per cent now remains.

●●●●●●● ➤ IN FOCUS: Biodiversity 'Hot Spots'

Biodiversity means biological diversity – the variety of all forms of life on earth – plants, animals and micro-organisms. 'Hot spots' refer to small regions that have a high biodiversity or an important ecological value – the islands of Hawaii and the cloud forests of Costa Rica are both good examples because of their unique diversity of species. In Costa Rica, the cloud forest is home to over one hundred species of mammals, four hundred species of birds, one hundred and twenty species of reptiles and amphibians, and several thousand species of insect. Another example, the Klamath-Siskiyou temperate forest in Washington, contains thirty conifer species and one hundred and thirty-one plants, including the Brewer spruce, Port Orford cedar and the insect-eating cobra lily.

In many areas, environments are now protected to preserve their beauty, the plant and animal life they contain – and the tourist earnings they bring in.

The Monteverde Cloud Forest in Costa Rica is an example of a successfully managed ecotourism project. Ecotourism refers to tourism that respects the environment and the needs of local people. At Monteverde, tourist numbers have been limited to protect the cloud forest, and local people have benefited from their involvement in tourism – as hosts, as farmers, and by developing attractions such as riding stables, local crafts and butterfly farms. Up to one-quarter of Belize, including offshore areas, has been designated as a nature reserve in some form, including the Cockscombe Basin Wildlife Sanctuary and the Blue Hole National Park. Nevertheless, these parks still experience pressures from tourism, and from logging companies keen to exploit the tropical forests for their wood and other products (gums, resins and oils).

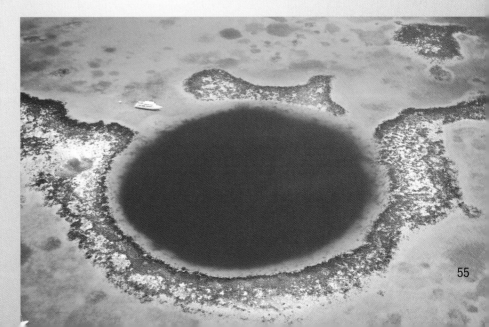

The Blue Hole is a sunken cave system surrounded by the Lighthouse Reef Atoll, off the coast of Belize.

FACT FILE

Coral off the coast of Montserrat has been killed by the ash and dust emitted by the Soufriére Hills volcano.

FACT FILE

Florida's coral reefs attract annual tourism revenues of over US$1.6 billion.

Coral reefs are often described as 'the rainforests of the sea' because of their great biodiversity.

CORAL REEFS

Coral reefs are often thought of as 'the rainforests of the sea' because of the huge number of species they contain and their vulnerability to destruction. Occupying less than 0.25 per cent of the marine environment, coral reefs nevertheless shelter more than 25 per cent of all known fish species.

Coral reefs are another ecological 'hot spot' and are experiencing severe pressures from modern development. Many of the Caribbean's coral reefs are under threat, with 29 per cent of them, such as those off Belize, Montserrat, Antigua, Jamaica and Puerto Rico, considered to be at high risk. Destruction takes many forms. For example, if the water above a coral reef becomes cloudy, the supply of light can be affected which can kill the coral. This cloudiness can be caused by road construction increasing run-off and carrying sediment into the sea, or by high levels of nutrients from agricultural areas or pollutants such as petroleum products. Increasing discharges of municipal waste also

decreases the quality of water, killing coral in the process. Large sections of coral reefs have been destroyed by boats dropping anchors or grounding. Moreover, a desire for souvenirs from increasing numbers of tourists also increases the commercial exploitation of reefs.

The peaks of the Pitons in Soufrière, St Lucia are some of the most recognizeable features in the Caribbean.

STRATEGIC PLANNING IN THE CARIBBEAN

Nearly all of the countries in the Caribbean have threatened ecosystems, and most have now developed plans to protect these environments. Non-government organizations (NGOs), including charities, are also increasingly involved in data-collection and public education. In St Lucia, for example, the National Trust now incorporates scientific data in the management of its national parks, including the Barre de Isle rainforest and the Soufrière Marine Management Area. Similarly, Bermuda has closed its pot-fishing industry to protect the island's biodiversity and its lucrative reef-based tourism.

●●●●●● ▶ IN FOCUS:
Folkestone Coral Reef, Barbados

The Folkestone Park and Marine Reserve was established in 1981 on the west coast of Barbados. The Reserve stretches a total distance of 2.2 km (1.4 miles) and extends a distance offshore of 950 m (3,117 feet) at its widest point and 660 m (2,165 feet) at its narrowest. Within the Reserve there are four well-developed fringing reefs (coral reefs that grow in shallow waters), several patch reefs (small reefs) and an offshore bank reef (growing on deep bottom irregularities). However, over-fishing, poor habitat quality and a severe disease that targeted reef fish in 1994 have all depleted the fish population. It is hoped that the diversity of fish will increase over time, although success has so far been slow.

9. THE FUTURE OF NORTH AMERICA

*T*HERE ARE MANY PROBLEMS THAT ARE LIKELY TO FACE North America in the future, and they vary from place to place. The physical environment provides many opportunities – but also some problems. Tectonic activity in the Caribbean and the western edge of North America remains a real threat. The risks from hurricane activity are increasing as more people live in vulnerable areas. Low-lying coastal communities on the eastern side of sub-tropical North America are most at risk from this damage.

FACT FILE

Up to 30 per cent of Mexico City's water is wasted through leakage and theft by individuals and organized gangs, who sell it to those people without water.

WATER

In some areas, such as the southwestern United States and Mexico, water shortages may increase as weather patterns change and as population growth causes a strain on scarce water resources. For example, the main source of water for Mexico City is an aquifer (water-bearing rock) which is running dry. Two-thirds of the city's water needs are supplied by this aquifer, the rest from reservoirs 120 km (75 miles) away, but the increasing demand on these distant water sources is bringing Mexico City into conflict with neighbouring states.

RESOURCES

Some natural resources, such as oil, will eventually run out and alternative forms of energy, such as HEP, solar and geothermal energy, are being developed. These energy sources are important for the sustainable growth of North America. Other resources have been over-exploited. The fate of the Canadian cod industry is a good example (see page 41). Nevertheless, the North American economy is large and strong and the immigration of skilled workers into North America, in particular to the

United States, will provide it with an advantage over most other continents in terms of research and development in the future.

ECONOMIES
Co-operation between smaller nations is likely to increase, in order to improve their trading options. Many smaller countries will try to vary their trading partners so that they have dealings with a range of countries in a variety of locations, such as Pacific Rim countries and European Union countries, as well as those within North America. More of the region's trade is likely to be with Asia, especially with China.

For many of the Caribbean countries, dependence on tourism is likely to increase. In Antigua, employment in farming is declining but employment in tourism is increasing. This shift may create advantages, such as investment and the growth of jobs, but it will require careful planning otherwise the disadvantages of environmental destruction, pollution and economic dependence will outweigh the advantages. There is a fine balancing act, and tourism needs to be sustainable, as is the case in Costa Rica and Belize (see page 55).

THE WORLD'S SUPERPOWER
In the United States, the continued battle against the rise of international terrorism, both at home and overseas, is a major issue. As the world's only superpower, the United States will continue to find that other countries look to it for help. At the same time, many may blame the United States for some of their problems when things go wrong. The United States has a unique, and uniquely difficult, role in the world of the future.

The World Trade Center light memorial – a tribute to the thousands who died, and a reminder of the work ahead in the years to come if there is to be global peace.

STATISTICAL COMPENDIUM

Sources: UN Agencies, World Bank and Britannica

Nation	Area (sq km)	Population (2003)	Urbanization (% population) 2003	Life expectancy at birth 2002 (in years)	GDP per capita (US$) 2002	Percentage of population under 15 years 2003	Percentage of population over 65 years 2003
Antigua and Barbuda	442	73,000	37.7	73.9	10,920	20	8
Aruba	193	100,000	45.4	N/a	N/a	N/a	N/a
Bahamas, The	13,939	314,000	89.5	67.1	17,280	28	6
Barbados	430	270,000	51.7	77.1	15,290	20	10
Belize	22,965	256,000	48.3	71.5	6,080	37	5
Bermuda	54	82,000	100.0	N/a	N/a	N/a	N/a
Canada	9,970,610	31,510,000	80.4	79.3	29,480	18	13
Costa Rica	51,100	4,173,000	60.6	78.0	8,840	30	6
Cuba	110,861	11,300,000	75.6	76.7	5,259	20	10
Dominica	750	79,000	72.0	73.1	5,640	25	8
Dominican Republic	48,671	8,745,000	59.3	66.7	6,640	32	5
El Salvador	21,041	6,515,000	59.6	70.6	4,890	35	5
Greenland	2,166,086	57,000	82.4	69.0	N/a	N/a	N/a
Grenada	344	80,000	40.7	65.3	7,280	34	8
Guadeloupe	1,780	440,000	99.7	N/a	N/a	N/a	N/a
Guatemala	108,889	12,347,000	46.3	65.7	4,080	42	3
Haiti	27,700	8,326,000	37.5	52.0	N/a	39	3
Honduras	112,492	6,941,000	45.6	68.8	2,600	41	3
Jamaica	10,991	2,651,000	52.1	75.6	3,980	30	7
Martinique	1,128	393,000	95.7	N/a	N/a	N/a	N/a
Mexico	1,958,201	103,457,000	75.5	73.3	8,970	32	5
Netherlands Antilles	800	221,000	69.7	76.0	N/a	23	9
Nicaragua	131,812	5,466,000	57.3	69.4	2,470	41	3
Panama	75,517	3,120,000	57.1	74.6	6,170	30	6
Puerto Rico	9,104	3,879,000	96.7	77.0	N/a	23	10
St Kitts and Nevis	269	42,000	32.2	70.0	12,420	26	11
St Lucia	617	149,000	30.5	72.4	5,300	31	6
St Vincent and the Grenadines	389	120,000	58.3	74.0	5,460	27	8
Trinidad and Tobago	5,128	1,303,000	75.4	71.4	9,430	24	6
United States	9,363,364	294,043,000	80.1	77.0	35,750	21	12
Virgin Islands (US)	352	111,000	93.6	78.0	N/a	25	9

GLOSSARY

Bauxite The main ore of aluminium.

Biodiversity Biological diversity – a measure of the variety of the earth's species, and the ecosystems that support these species.

Biomass Plant matter or other biodegradable material that can be used in various ways to make fuel.

Cash crop A crop that is grown for sale.

Civil rights movement A movement that campaigns for equal rights for black citizens.

Commonwealth (British) An association of independent countries which were formerly part of the British Empire.

Communism Revolutionary socialism that emphasizes common ownership of the means of production and the principle that everyone should work according to their capacity and receive according to their needs.

Conquistadors ('conquerors') The early Spanish explorers and colonists who conquered large parts of Central America.

Conurbation An extensive built-up area formed by the merging of cities.

Cordillera A series of mountain ranges that run broadly parallel to each other, and relate to a single mountain-building period.

Democracy A system of government in which representatives are chosen by the people in free elections.

Denomination A group within a particular faith that emphasizes a particular aspect of that faith.

Dictator An absolute ruler who is often not elected.

Ecosystem An integrated unit consisting of plants and animals, and the environment in which they live.

Ecotourism Tourism that respects the environment and the needs of local people.

El Niño A warm ocean current that periodically appears in the Pacific Ocean, disrupting the normal circulation and causing widespread climatic disorder, for example floods and droughts.

European Union (EU) A political and economic alliance of European countries.

Federal A system of government in which power is held by both national and regional governments.

Fossil fuels Fuels such as coal, oil and natural gas, formed from the fossilized remains of plants that lived hundreds of millions of years ago.

Free trade Trade between countries without controls such as tariffs or taxes.

Genocide The deliberate murder of a specific group of people.

Geothermal Energy derived from heated rocks beneath the earth's surface.

Ghetto A densely populated, deprived area in a city.

Global warming The gradual warming of the earth's atmosphere, largely as a result of the burning of fossil fuels.

Gross Domestic Product (GDP) The total earnings of a country from sources within that country.

Groundwater Water that is held in porous rocks and soils in the ground.

Hydroelectric power (HEP) Power generated by the energy of moving water.

Ice Age A period of time in the earth's history when temperatures were lower, and ice sheets covered more of the earth's surface.

Indigenous Describes the native people of an area.

Latino A person of Latin American origin – that is from Central America and the Caribbean.

Maquiladoras Industries in Mexico, located along the US border, which take advantage of cheap supplies of labour and lax environmental legislation.

Permeable Describes something that can be penetrated by liquid.

Pyroclastic flows Clouds of superheated ash and gas from an erupting volcano.

Renewable energy Power from a source of energy that can be used over and over again and will not run out.

Richter Scale A scale for measuring the energy released by an earthquake.

Runoff Water that flows over the ground rather than soaking into it.

Sanction A penalty imposed by one country against another.

Shanty town A poor area of a town or city where people live in flimsy dwellings, often without access to adequate sanitation.

Subsidy Financial aid, often given by a government.

Superpower A state that through its economic or political power can dominate smaller countries.

Tectonics The movement of the earth's crustal plates and the resulting effects such as volcanic activity, earthquakes, folding and faulting.

Tundra Treeless plain consisting of grasses, sedge, heather, moss and lichens, found at high latitudes and high altitudes.

Urbanization The proportion of people living in urban areas.

FURTHER INFORMATION

BOOKS TO READ:

North America J.H. Paterson (Oxford University Press, 1994)

The Caribbean Environment Mark Wilson (Oxford University Press, 2005)

The Changing Face of Mexico Edward Parker (Wayland, 2004)

The Changing Face of the Caribbean Ali Brownlie (Wayland, 2006)

The USA (Horrible Histories series) Terry Deary (Scholastic, 2001)

USA Olly Phillipson (Heinemann, 2000)

USEFUL WEBSITES:

http://www.cia.gov/cia/publications/factbook/index.html
The CIA World Factbook, an excellent source of information on all countries in the world.

http://911digitalarchive.org/
A website dedicated to the events of 11 September 2001. It is an evocative, moving site and well worth time spent over its resources.

http://www.eia.doe.gov/emeu/cabs/nonopec.html
A good source of data on oil production with good links to regional production of oil

http://www.caribbean-on-line.com/
A useful portal to discover some of the attractions and charms of the Caribbean.

INDEX

ABOUT THE AUTHOR

Dr Garrett Nagle has written a number of geography textbooks and articles from primary school level to university level. His doctorate was at the University of Oxford, and he has taught in Oxford for the last twenty years.